BIRTH OF THE STAR-SPANGLED BANNER

A FLY on the WALL HISTORY

O say can you see, by the dawn's early light,
What so proudly we hail'd at the twilight's last gleaming,
Whose broad stripes and bright stars through the perilous fight
O'er the ramparts we watch'd were so gallantly stream

And the rocket's red glare, the bombs bursting in air,
Gave proof through the night that our flag was still there,
O say does that star-spangled banner yet wave
O'er the land of the free and the home of the brave?

BY THOMAS KINGSLEY TROUPE   ILLUSTRATED BY JOMIKE TEJIDO

PICTURE WINDOW BOOKS
a capstone imprint

Hi, I'm Horace, and this is my sister, Maggie.

We've been "flies on the wall" during important events in history.

We watched workers carve the Great Sphinx of Giza in ancient Egypt.

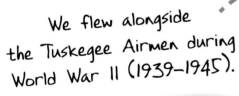

We even walked on the moon with Neil Armstrong!

We flew alongside the Tuskegee Airmen during World War II (1939–1945).

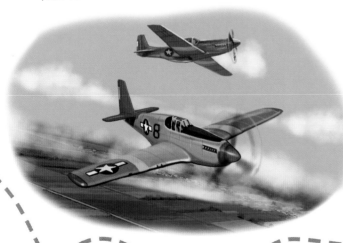

One thing we didn't expect to see was the birth of our national anthem . . .

Maggie and I were buzzing around Washington, D.C., in August 1814. The United States was at war with Great Britain. The two countries were fighting over many things, including trade issues and maritime rights. British troops had just captured and burned the U.S. capital.

Soldiers filled the streets. Fires smoldered everywhere. Maggie and I were scared. What would happen to our country?

* * *

The conflict with Great Britain was known as the War of 1812.

* * *

My sister and I wanted to escape the danger, so we slipped through an open window of a small building. It was the office of lawyer Francis Scott Key. A man named Richard West was talking to him. Both men looked worried.

British soldiers had thrown a friend of theirs, Dr. William Beanes, in jail. Richard had come to Francis for help.

Francis Scott Key seems like more than a lawyer.

Don't those look like poems on his desk?

Maybe he writes to keep his mind off the war.

This was a long time before people had TV and movies, you know!

✳ ✳ ✳

Francis Scott Key was born on August 1, 1779. He and his wife, Mary, married in 1802 and had 11 children together.

✳ ✳ ✳

5

Richard said that Dr. Beanes and his friends caught a few British soldiers looting houses in their neighborhood. The men worked together to have the soldiers thrown in jail.

But one of the soldiers escaped. He told British general Robert Ross what had happened. Having his soldiers jailed made General Ross angry. He gave orders to have Dr. Beanes arrested. British soldiers showed up at night and pulled the doctor out of bed. They took him away as a prisoner.

They're taking Dr. Beanes away in the middle of the night?

I hope they let him change out of his pajamas.

I think being in his pajamas is the least of Dr. Beanes' problems, Horace!

* * *

Dr. Beanes was awoken around midnight and taken to a British camp. He was then moved onto a British warship outside Baltimore, Maryland. His friends asked that he be released, but the British refused.

* * *

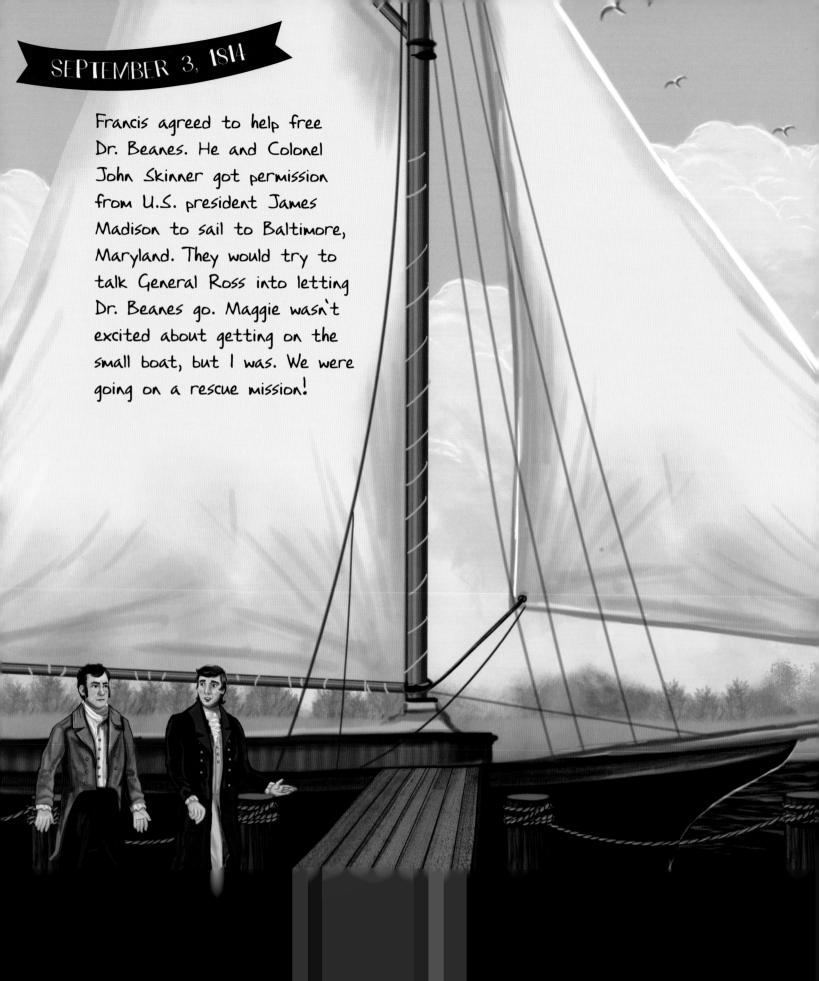

Francis agreed to help free Dr. Beanes. He and Colonel John Skinner got permission from U.S. president James Madison to sail to Baltimore, Maryland. They would try to talk General Ross into letting Dr. Beanes go. Maggie wasn't excited about getting on the small boat, but I was. We were going on a rescue mission!

After a few days, we came upon the British warship HMS Tonnant. Francis raised a white flag. It told the British soldiers that he just wanted to talk.

That British ship is huge!

Let's hope the people on board are friendly.

I just hope Dr. Beanes hasn't been hurt!

★ ★ ★

The letters *HMS* on British ships are an abbreviation. They stand for "His/Her Majesty's Ship," which means the ship sails for the king or queen of England.

★ ★ ★

General Ross and his officers were mostly friendly to Francis and Colonel Skinner. They talked and invited them to have dinner aboard the ship. But when Francis asked if the British would free Dr. Beanes, they said no.

That's when Francis handed over a stack of letters. The letters were from wounded British soldiers. They explained how well Dr. Beanes had treated the men and cared for their wounds.

Wow! I'm glad we have those letters.

It just might help!

You're right.

Being kind to others usually gets you farther than being mean.

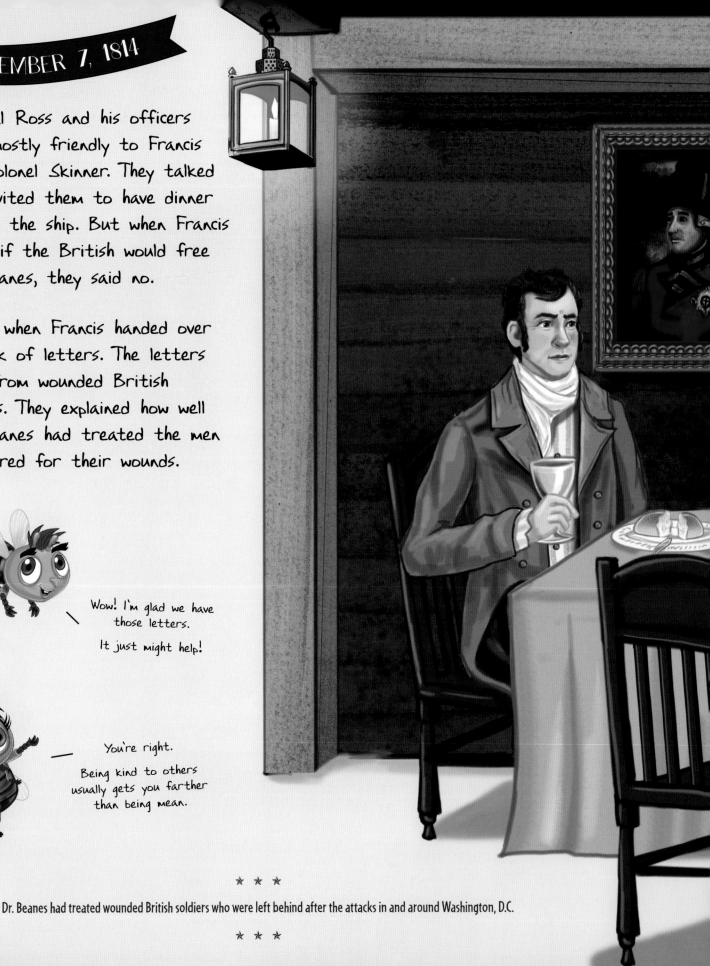

＊ ＊ ＊

Dr. Beanes had treated wounded British soldiers who were left behind after the attacks in and around Washington, D.C.

＊ ＊ ＊

General Ross read the letters and changed his mind about
Dr. Beanes. He agreed to let the doctor go. Maggie and
I couldn't believe it! The mission was a success! We could
all return home and live happily ever after.

But . . . there was a catch.

British troops had an attack planned on Baltimore's Fort McHenry. They couldn't let their guests from the United States leave until the attack was over. So Francis, Dr. Beanes, and Colonel Skinner were ordered to sit on their small boat, under British guard — and wait.

Well, this is weird.

We're just supposed to wait while the British attack one of our forts?

I guess so, Maggie.

I think the British officers are worried that Francis and his friends overheard their plans.

They don't want the Americans to warn anyone about the attack.

Early in the morning, a large number of British warships began their attack. Cannons thundered. Bombs exploded. BOOM! BOOM! BOOM! Maggie and I covered our ears. I couldn't imagine how loud it was over at Fort McHenry!

Francis and the others watched. All we could do was hope the soldiers at Fort McHenry survived the bombing. The fort had to stand and protect the city of Baltimore.

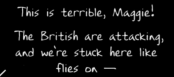

This is terrible, Maggie!

The British are attacking, and we're stuck here like flies on —

On flypaper? I know!

The U.S. flag is still waving, but who knows for how long.

Around 1,800 bombs were fired at Fort McHenry during the British attack.

* * *

The attack on Fort McHenry lasted all day. The Americans fought back hard. They sunk a few British ships. Still, everyone on our boat seemed to think Fort McHenry was doomed.

Maggie and I tried to get a good look inside the fort, but it was much too dangerous to fly. Bombs rained from the sky. So did actual rain!

★ ★ ★

During the battle, a rainstorm hit the coast. Soldiers replaced Fort McHenry's regular flag with a smaller "storm" flag. They didn't want the larger flag to catch the wind and break the flagpole.

★ ★ ★

Once night fell, the battle stopped. All was quiet. Everyone on our boat went belowdecks to get some rest. Maggie and I thought the fighting was over. Finally!

But sometime in the middle of the night, cannons started firing again. BOOM! BOOM! BOOM! Smaller British warships had moved closer to shore. Francis stayed up the entire night to listen and watch.

✶ ✶ ✶

The rockets the British fired weighed 32 pounds (15 kilograms) each. They had lit fuses and were supposed to explode when they hit their target. Many of the rockets never reached Fort McHenry.

✶ ✶ ✶

As the sun rose, we all looked toward Fort McHenry. The big U.S. flag was flying high in the early-morning sky. After bombing for 25 hours, the British ships finally gave up the fight. They started sailing away.

* * *

The flag flying above Fort McHenry was 42 feet (13 meters) wide by 30 feet (9 m) tall.
It was big enough for every ship in the harbor to see from a distance.

* * *

With the fighting stopped, Maggie and I flew across the harbor to visit Fort McHenry. The fort was pretty beat up, but it was still standing.

The men cheered. They'd fought long and hard. A few of their fellow soldiers had been killed. Some were wounded. But the battle was a victory for the United States. The Americans had won the Battle of Baltimore!

These men are super brave, Maggie.

I mean, just the sounds of the cannons scared me.

I agree. Hopefully now the soldiers can take a break — and maybe a nap!

Four U.S. soldiers died during the battle, and 24 were wounded.

Maggie and I buzzed back to the boat to see what Francis and his friends were up to. Francis had pulled an old letter from his pocket. He was writing on the back of it.

O say can you see, by the dawn's early light,

What so proudly we hail'd at the twilight's last gleaming,

Whose broad stripes and bright stars through the perilous fight

O'er the ramparts we watch'd were so gallantly streaming?

★ ★ ★

The word *ramparts* means the walls of a fort. In Francis Scott Key's poem, the word is used to describe Fort McHenry.

★ ★ ★

I knew it, Horace!

Francis isn't just a lawyer.

He's a poet too!

Cool! It looks like he's writing about seeing the flag over Fort McHenry this morning.

And how it was still flying high after the dangerous fighting last night.

25

Once we reached Baltimore, Francis headed for a hotel. He worked more on his poem. He described the color of the British rockets when they lit up the sky. He wrote about how he could see the U.S. flag flying all night. And he proudly called the United States "the land of the free and the home of the brave."

★ ★ ★

The Baltimore Patriot printed Francis' poem on September 20, 1814. It was called "Defence of Fort M'Henry."

★ ★ ★

I think Francis is in love with that flag, Maggie!

I think so too, Horace.

It's like the flag isn't flying over just Fort McHenry.

It's waving over the entire country!

O say can you see, by the dawn's early light,

What so proudly we hail'd at the twilight's last gleaming,

Whose broad stripes and bright stars through the perilous fight

O'er the ramparts we watch'd were so gallantly streaming?

And the rocket's red glare, the bombs bursting in air,

Gave proof through the night that our flag was still there,

O say does that star-spangled banner yet wave

O'er the land of the free and the home of the brave?

Francis Scott Key's finished poem was four stanzas, or sections, long. It was printed in newspapers and later set to music to a tune called "To Anacreon in Heaven." Americans soon began calling the song "The Star-Spangled Banner." It became the national anthem of the United States of America in 1931. Usually, only the first verse is sung.

* * *

The Fort McHenry flag is displayed at the Smithsonian National Museum of American History in Washington, D.C.

* * *

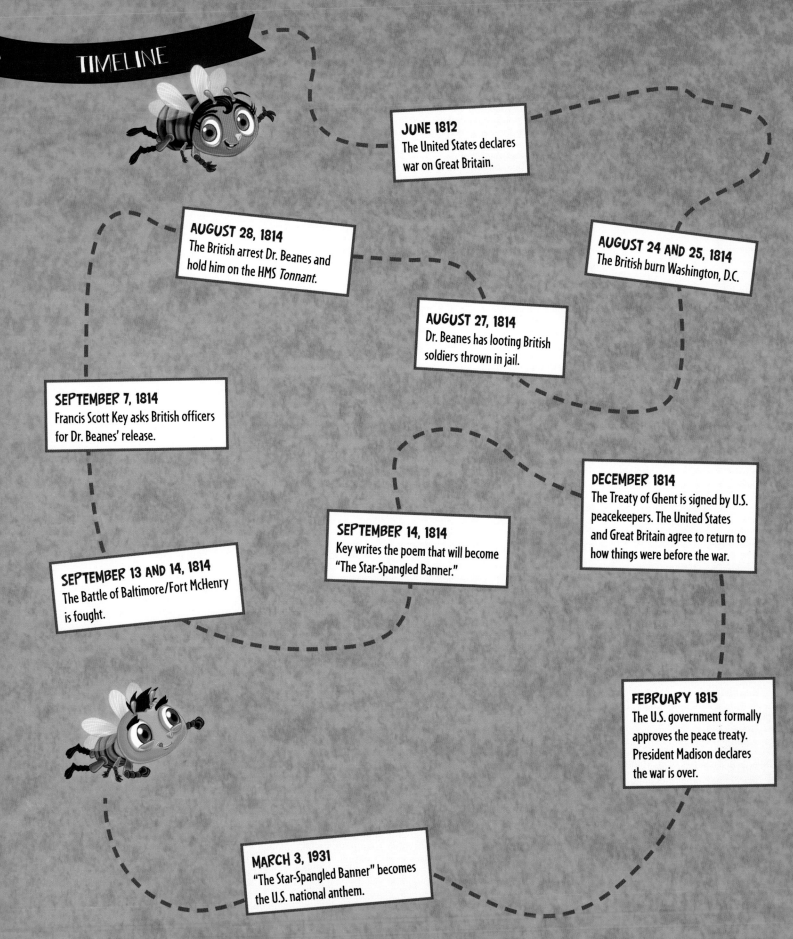

TIMELINE

JUNE 1812
The United States declares war on Great Britain.

AUGUST 24 AND 25, 1814
The British burn Washington, D.C.

AUGUST 28, 1814
The British arrest Dr. Beanes and hold him on the HMS *Tonnant*.

AUGUST 27, 1814
Dr. Beanes has looting British soldiers thrown in jail.

SEPTEMBER 7, 1814
Francis Scott Key asks British officers for Dr. Beanes' release.

DECEMBER 1814
The Treaty of Ghent is signed by U.S. peacekeepers. The United States and Great Britain agree to return to how things were before the war.

SEPTEMBER 14, 1814
Key writes the poem that will become "The Star-Spangled Banner."

SEPTEMBER 13 AND 14, 1814
The Battle of Baltimore/Fort McHenry is fought.

FEBRUARY 1815
The U.S. government formally approves the peace treaty. President Madison declares the war is over.

MARCH 3, 1931
"The Star-Spangled Banner" becomes the U.S. national anthem.

GLOSSARY

arrest–to stop and hold someone for doing something against the law

deck–a floor on a ship

fuse–a cord or wick that can burn from end to end

gallantly–bravely

lawyer–a person who is trained to advise people about the law

loot–to steal from stores or houses during wartime or after a disaster

maritime–related to the sea, ships, or sea travel

mission–a planned job or task

national anthem–a song expressing a particular country's pride

officer–someone who is in charge of other people

perilous–dangerous

rampart–the surrounding wall of a fort built to protect against attack

spangled–covered with sparkle

troop–a group of soldiers

THINK ABOUT IT

1. Step by step, describe the events that led to the arrest of Dr. William Beanes.

2. Francis Scott Key gave General Ross a stack of letters written by wounded British soldiers. Why were those letters so important to getting Dr. Beanes released from jail?

3. Using the glossary and the illustrations in this book, explain what the first eight lines of "The Star-Spangled Banner" mean.

READ MORE

Radomski, Kassandra. *Mr. Madison's War: Causes and Effects of the War of 1812.* Cause and Effect. North Mankato, Minn.: Capstone Press, a Capstone Imprint, 2014.

Rustad, Martha E. H. *Why Are There Stripes on the American Flag?* Our American Symbols. Minneapolis: Millbrook Press, 2015.

Stewart, Gabrielle. *That Star-Spangled Banner: The War, the Flag, and the National Anthem.* Largo, Md.: Generation A, 2015.

INTERNET SITES

Use FactHound to find Internet sites related to this book:

Visit *www.facthound.com*

Just type in 9781515816010 and go.

Check out projects, games and lots more at
www.capstonekids.com

INDEX

Look for other books in the series:

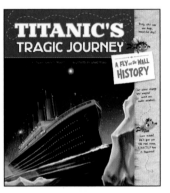

Special thanks to our adviser, Kevin Byrne, PhD, Professor Emeritus of History, Gustavus Adolphus College, for his expertise.

Picture Window Books is published by Capstone,
1710 Roe Crest Drive, North Mankato, Minnesota 56003
www.mycapstone.com

Library of Congress Cataloging-in-Publication data is available on the Library of Congress website.
ISBN 978-1-5158-1601-0 (library binding)
ISBN 978-1-5158-1605-8 (paperback)
ISBN 978-1-5158-1609-6 (eBook PDF)

Summary: Describes the events leading up to and including the bombing of Fort McHenry during the War of 1812, which inspired Francis Scott Key to pen the words to the U.S. national anthem, "The Star-Spangled Banner."

Editor: Jill Kalz
Designer: Sarah Bennett
Creative Director: Nathan Gassman
Production Specialist: Laura Manthe

The illustrations in this book were planned with pencil on paper and finished with digital paints.

Printed and bound in the United States of America.
002559

Published by Princeton Architectural Press
A McEvoy Group company
202 Warren Street, Hudson, NY 12534
www.papress.com

First published in France under the title: *Mon Île*
© 2018 La Martinière Jeunesse, a division of La Martinière Groupe, Paris

English edition © 2019 Princeton Architectural Press
All rights reserved
Printed and bound in China
22 21 20 19 4 3 2 1 First edition

ISBN 978-1-61689-813-7

Princeton Architectural Press is a leading publisher in architecture,
design, photography, landscape, and visual culture. We create
fine books and stationery of unsurpassed quality and production
values. With more than one thousand titles published, we find
design everywhere and in the most unlikely places.

No part of this book may be used or reproduced in any manner
without written permission from the publisher, except in the context
of reviews.

Every reasonable attempt has been made to identify owners of
copyright. Errors or omissions will be corrected in subsequent editions.

This book was illustrated using watercolors, colored pencils,
and red thread.

For Princeton Architectural Press:
Editor: Nina Pick
Typesetting: Benjamin English

Special thanks to: Paula Baver, Janet Behning, Abby Bussel,
Jan Cigliano Hartman, Susan Hershberg, Kristen Hewitt, Lia Hunt,
Valerie Kamen, Jennifer Lippert, Sara McKay, Parker Menzimer,
Eliana Miller, Wes Seeley, Rob Shaeffer, Sara Stemen, Marisa Tesoro,
Paul Wagner, and Joseph Weston of Princeton Architectural Press
–Kevin C. Lippert, publisher

Library of Congress Cataloging-in-Publication Data available
from the publisher upon request.

To all children, young and old,
who are overflowing with imagination,
especially Ondine and Maixent.
S. S. R.

To Léna, whose beautiful imagination
and beautiful houses inspired this story.
To Anouck and the lovely songs
she invents and hums.
S. D.-P.

MY ISLAND

Text by Stéphanie Demasse-Pottier

Illustrations by Seng Soun Ratanavanh

Princeton Architectural Press
New York

I live on an island that has no name,

an island where the flowers are always blooming,

an island where there are thousands of birds,

and other animals, including snails.

Sometimes my friends come to visit,
we have lunch on plastic dishes.

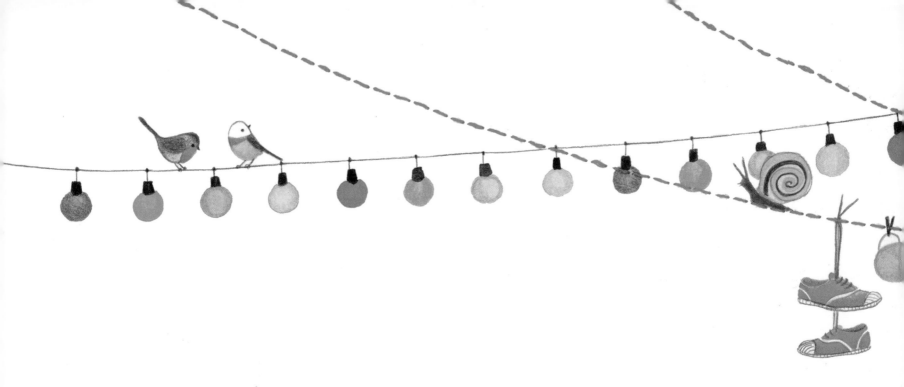

I have a house too. Inside, there are flowers, colorful plates,
a hanging coffeemaker, strange bric-a-brac.

I spend hours and hours in my house.
There's always something to do there, a snail to tame,
a bouquet of flowers to arrange.

Inside my house, on my island, I feel at home.
There is no door, you can come in.

You too are welcome on my island
if you know how to sing,

if you know how to share,

if you know how to dream.

Stephanie Demasse-Pottier works as a librarian
specializing in children's books. She lives near Paris.
She is also the author of *Too Bad for the Rain,
Louise, My Little Collection of Summer Memories,*
and *The Disappearance of Chou.*
My Island is her first book to appear in English.

Seng Soun Ratanavanh is a painter and illustrator
based in Paris. She graduated from
the School of Fine Arts in Paris.
She is the illustrator of the award-winning
Miyuki books.